Puerto Rico

in pictures

Students at the University of Puerto Rico. College enrollment on the island has more than doubled in the last 10 years—to 35,000 students—at all the universities in Puerto Rico.

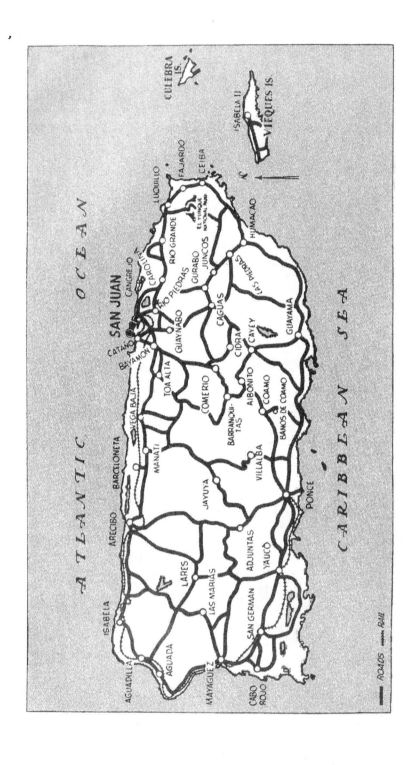

Puerto Rico

in pictures

Luquillo Beach

VISUAL GEOGRAPHY SERIES

STERLING PUBLISHING CO., INC. *New York*

The Oak Tree Press
LONDON AND MELBOURNE

VISUAL GEOGRAPHY SERIES

Alaska	Guatemala	Puerto Rico
Australia	Hawaii	Russia
Austria	Holland	Scotland
Belgium and Luxembourg	Hong Kong	Spain
Berlin—East and West	India	Sweden
Canada	Ireland	Switzerland
Ceylon	Israel	Tahiti and the
Chile	Italy	French Islands of
Denmark	Japan	the Pacific
England	Malaysia and Singapore	Thailand
Finland	Mexico	Turkey
France	New Zealand	Venezuela
French Canada	Peru	Wales
Ghana	The Philippines	Yugoslavia
Greece	Portugal	

Prepared by
ROBERT V. MASTERS

ACKNOWLEDGMENTS

The publishers wish to thank the Economic Development Administration of the Commonwealth of Puerto Rico for their advice and assistance, as well as for many of the photographs used in this book. Grateful acknowledgment also is made to the Puerto Rico News Service who have graciously provided the majority of the photographs, and to Pan American World Airways for the photograph at the top of page 23.

Sixth Printing, 1966

Revised Edition © 1965, © 1961 by
Sterling Publishing Co., Inc.
419 Park Avenue South, New York, N.Y. 10016
Published in Great Britain and the Commonwealth in 1966
by Oak Tree Press, Ltd., 116, Baker Street, London, W.1
All rights reserved
Manufactured in the United States of America

Library of Congress Catalog Card No.: 61-10399

CONTENTS

From the ramparts of El Morro, shown here, the Spanish successfully battled Sir Francis Drake and his fleet, repelled an invasion by the Dutch and withstood a siege by an English expedition numbering 10,000 men.

INTRODUCTION

Puerto Rico has had a vivid, sometimes violent, sometimes glamorous past. The island's history brings to mind the daring voyages of the first Spanish explorers and settlers, the names of Ponce de León and of Sir Francis Drake who attacked the colony, and visions of lawless pirates who sailed the Caribbean in search of foreign vessels to raid. From the time of the island's discovery by Columbus in 1493 until Puerto Rico achieved the status of a Commonwealth of the United States in 1952, she was dominated by foreign powers and denied the right to govern herself.

Throughout their turbulent history, Puerto Ricans themselves seldom benefitted from the riches of their island. Gold, sugar cane, timber, tropical fruits—her natural products were developed and marketed by outside powers, first by Spain and, later, by the United States. Even after Puerto Rico became a United States possession in 1898 as a result of the Spanish-American War, the island remained poor. Educational facilities, though improved, remained inadequate, and islanders had only a small measure of political autonomy. They could not elect their own government nor control their own schools.

In 1938 this situation began to change rapidly. In that year Luís Muñoz Marín organized the Popular Democratic Party. Under the leadership of Muñoz, Puerto Rico's first elected Governor, the island made astonishing advances in industry, agriculture, housing, education and other areas of social importance. Today, for example, the Commonwealth spends a larger proportion of its national budget on education than does any other country in the world except Israel. Illiteracy has been practically eliminated. Slums are being cleared, overnight it seems, and replaced by attractive, inexpensive housing. The tourist industry has become "big business." And no wonder! With the magnificent, varied scenery which includes tropical rain forests, wide fine-grained sand beaches, steep mountains covered with greenery, thick bushes and trees, vivid flowers in every color imaginable and an average temperature in the 70°'s, Puerto Rico is both beautiful and comfortable. As Governor Muñoz predicted when he named his scheme for economic and social reform "Operation Bootstrap," Puerto Ricans are turning their island into a dynamic and prosperous country. And they have done this without sacrificing the graceful traditions of the past—the gentle charm of old Spain is still reflected in the architecture, music, poetry and gracious customs of Puerto Rico.

This monument marks the spot near Aguadilla on Puerto Rico's west coast where Columbus is thought to have landed in 1493. Two other cities in the area also claim to be the original landing place of the Italian explorer who discovered the island on his second voyage to the New World.

I. PUERTO RICO'S HISTORY

The history of Puerto Rico is typical of the history of all the islands in the Caribbean Sea. It was discovered by Columbus, exploited by the Spanish, repeatedly attacked by the English and used as a base by pirates and smugglers.

Called *Borinquén* by its native Indians, Puerto Rico (rich port) was discovered by Columbus on his second voyage to the New World in 1493. Columbus renamed the island San Juan Bautista (St. John the Baptist). Although he ordered a few herds of cattle sent over from the Spanish colony of Hispaniola (the present-day Dominican Republic) to fatten in the island's lush valleys, no serious effort at colonization was made until 1508.

In that year King Ferdinand of Spain sent Juan Ponce de León, who had been a foot soldier with Columbus, to the island. Ponce arrived with 50 armed men, an inhumane attitude towards the island's 30,000 Indians, a thirst for gold and grand ideas of forming a new Caribbean jewel for the crown of Spain.

Initially, Ponce was successful. The Indians, called the Arawaks or, sometimes, the Borinquéns, were close cousins of the savage Caribs found throughout the Caribbean, but seemed to lack their fierceness. They were quickly subdued and put to work in the gold mines. By 1582 the Arawaks had been worked to death; they disappeared altogether from the island's population.

The first Spanish settlement, Caparra, was started near what is now the city of San Juan. However, in 1519 Caparra was relocated to the present site of San Juan and was renamed Puerto Rico. How the city of Puerto Rico came to be called San Juan in 1521, and the island of San Juan to be known as Puerto Rico is a problem that still baffles historians. One theory is that a mapmaker inadvertently reversed the names. Except for a brief period from 1900 until 1932 when the island was mistakenly spelled "Porto Rico" by outsiders, its name has remained unchanged from 1521 until the present.

In the beginning, trade with Spain was brisk. In 1515 sugar cane was introduced from Santo Domingo, and a few years later the first Negro slaves were brought to the island to do the work formerly handled by the Arawaks. With slavery the custom, agriculture flourished. Cotton, ginger, cacao (chocolate), sugar cane and indigo (used in making blue dyes) were cultivated and exported in small quantities. In the first years of Spanish settlement a great deal of gold was mined.

However, the success of the new colony was to be short-lived. The gold mines, which yielded $4 (or £1½) million, were soon worked out. Nevertheless, Puerto Rico seemed a rich prize to the European powers, fiercely competing to add overseas possessions to their empires. France, England and even Holland tried to seize Puerto Rico from Spain. Until about 1580 the island was a target for French raiders. Striking mostly at unguarded settlements along the south, west and north coasts, they virtually stripped the island of its produce and cattle. These raids showed the Spanish the

9

A dramatic view of El Morro is obtained from the tiny Isla de Cabra, across the bay from Old San Juan. Incidentally, the crumbling pillars of this once-stately building show the method of construction used by the Spanish: a stucco facing applied to a brick foundation.

strategic importance of Puerto Rico. As a result, they fortified it. El Morro, a massive hulking fortress overlooking the port of San Juan, is still standing.

Following the French attacks on Puerto Rico were those of the English. In 1595, Sir Francis Drake launched a bloody but unsuccessful attack against El Morro. Three years later, George Clifford, the Earl of Cumberland, captured the fortress and held it for six months.

On a knoll overlooking the plaza of San German is Porta Coelli, believed to be the oldest Christian church in the western hemisphere. San German was settled in 1512 on the south coast, but was moved to its present site in 1570. It was one of the first settlements on the island in the early years of colonization.

But in 1598 a plague, one of several contagious and often fatal pulmonary diseases, ravaged the island. This, combined with the harassing counterattacks of the settlers, finally forced Clifford to withdraw.

Thirty years later it was the Dutch who tried to seize Puerto Rico. Boudwijn Hendrikszoon landed with a large force in 1624 and laid siege to El Morro for several weeks before he and his Dutch West Indies Company fleet were turned away.

Hendrikszoon's was the last foreign invasion for over 100 years, but during the 17th and 18th centuries the settlers found themselves endangered from still another quarter—Spain herself. European powers prized their colonies as markets for goods produced in the mother country. Therefore, under the rule of autocratic Castille, Puerto Rico was not allowed to

trade with any country except Spain—even though for years the Spanish merchants that plied the Caribbean had been bypassing the island for more lucrative ports.

French, Dutch, Danish and English traders, barred from engaging in legal trade with the Puerto Ricans, turned to smuggling their goods into the growing agricultural settlements along the coasts safely distant from San Juan. Slaves, farm equipment and cloth were exchanged for cattle, pigs, mules, ginger, tobacco, fruit, vegetables and, after 1750, coffee. Although smugglers flourished, contributing to the island's agricultural growth, trade in San Juan languished to the point of being nonexistent.

The one profitable enterprise established in San Juan during the 18th century was piracy. Supported by Spain, acting under letters of marque which asserted Spain's right to retaliate

11

This aerial view shows how the massive fortress of El Morro, built in 1539, stands guard at the entrance to San Juan. El Morro means the "headland."

by seizing the goods of other nations, privateers from Puerto Rico raided the trade lanes of the Caribbean. For more than 50 years they operated with savage efficiency and a blithe disregard for law. They were not a pleasant group, but they brought in the only wealth to be seen in San Juan during their day. As a result, privateers wielded a strong influence over the island and for many years played an active part in the government of the colony.

In 1797, after Spain had joined the French in hostilities against England, these same privateers helped government troops throw back a British force of 10,000 men who, under Lieutenant-General Sir Ralph Abercromby, had laid siege to El Morro.

Abercromby's failure was followed by almost a century of relative peace and gradual improvement of social, economic and political conditions. Alejandro Ramirez, a Spanish governor, took firm steps to abolish contraband trade in 1813, and in 1815, Spain permitted Puerto Rico to conduct unrestricted trade with foreign ships. This meant that Puerto Rico was open to immigration and settlement. The end of Spanish exclusivism brought settlers by the thousands to man the coffee plantations. From a population of 155,000 in 1800, Puerto Rico grew to 500,000 in 1850 and to 900,000 in 1898.

In spite of Spain's gradual willingness to permit the Puerto Ricans to govern themselves, small rebellions occurred in 1835, 1838, 1867 and 1868. Spain responded by giving Puerto Rico the status of a province in 1869, and at this time islanders became divided into two groups; those who liked the status quo and were satisfied with Spanish rule opposed the Liberals, or Autonomists, whose goal was

El Morro is long remembered by all visitors to Puerto Rico. Beneath its forbidding walls is a surprise—a modern nine-hole golf course. And from the ramparts of the fort, the trim cruising steamships of the Caribbean can be seen.

This monument marks the spot at Guanica on the south coast where the United States Marines landed during the Spanish-American War in 1898. The U.S. Marines met almost no opposition from the small Spanish garrison on Puerto Rico and captured the island easily.

13

This is the ancient fortress of San Geronimo, built by the Spanish in 1771 to protect the island from the raids of the European colonial powers and from pirates. It is now an arms museum. Located across the water is the luxurious Condado Beach section of San Juan. Condado Beach is covered with fine hotels, lavish night clubs and beautiful homes and apartment houses. In the distance, nearly hidden by floating cloud banks, are the mountains that run north to south, dividing the island.

Puerto Rican self-rule under the protection of Spain. .

Just as modern-day Puerto Rico owes a vast and inestimable debt to Governor Luís Muñoz Marín, 19th-century Puerto Rico was indebted to his father, Luís Muñoz Rivera, leader of the Autonomist Party. Largely because of his efforts in negotiating with Spain's liberal prime

Fort San-Cristobal dates back to 1631 when it was built by the Spanish to protect San Juan from land invasions. The handsome white domed building in the background is Puerto Rico's capitol.

minister, Práxedes Mateo Sagasta, Puerto Rico gained a large measure of independence during the latter part of the 19th century. Slavery was officially abolished in 1873. And in 1897 Puerto Rico was granted an autonomic Constitution.

No one knows whether Puerto Rico would have been unconditionally self-governing under this constitution. On July 25, 1898, shortly after the outbreak of the Spanish-American War, United States troops landed at Guanica on the southern coast. Although San Juan was bombed and there were a few minor skirmishes between defending Spanish troops and those of the Americans, the island fell with hardly a shot. In December of the same year, the Treaty of Paris ceded Puerto Rico to the United States.

At first the island had very little political freedom; the governor and all other top administrative officials were appointed by the President of the United States. Even harder on the island was the fact that the Federal government permitted economic exploitation by non-islanders. As a result, Puerto Ricans were still unable to advance economically or socially.

Beginning in 1940 Puerto Ricans began to change their situation. Under the aggressive leadership of Luís Muñoz Marín, who headed the newly formed Popular Democratic Party, Puerto Ricans began to fight for political independence and for a higher standard of living. In 1952 the island became a Commonwealth, for the first time in her history fully independent. Muñoz became its first elected Governor in 1948, serving until 1964, when he voluntarily stepped down from office. He was succeeded by Roberto Sanchez Vilella, who received 60 per cent of the popular vote in the 1964 election.

A walk along these ancient walls, which once protected San Juan from attacks by pirates, provides an excellent view of the waters surrounding Puerto Rico's capital city. Centuries ago travellers disembarked here. The sentry posts are part of La Fortaleza, the oldest governor's mansion in use today in the New World.

Parts of Old San Juan have recently been restored to preserve the area's delicate Spanish charm. The buildings shown here are located on Calle Cristo, one of Puerto Rico's oldest streets, and are especially attractive examples of 19th-century Spanish architecture.

Tropical skies, huge shade trees and clear streams are typical of the island's interior. The town in the distance is San German, one of the oldest on the island.

2. THE LAND

Running from near Key West, Florida, almost to South America, is a rugged chain of submerged mountains whose highest peaks have pushed above the water to form an erratic chain of islands known as the West Indies. Within the West Indies group Cuba, Jamaica, Haiti and Puerto Rico comprise what is known as the Greater Antilles. Puerto Rico is the easternmost and the smallest of the Greater Antilles, 1,050 miles from the tip of Florida. North of the island is the Atlantic Ocean; to the south lies the Caribbean Sea.

Approximately 100 miles long and 35 miles wide, the island has 3,435 square miles, an area twice the size of Trinidad but smaller than Jamaica. Into this compact area are jammed 2.6 million people, approximately 740 to each square mile—a population concentration greater than

Britain's and almost fifteen times that of the United States.

When asked by Queen Isabella to describe Puerto Rico, Columbus reportedly crumpled a piece of parchment and tossed it on the table as an illustration. Indeed, the island does look like a crumpled piece of stiff paper with jagged peaks, steep valleys and uneven plains. Two mountain chains cross the island from east to west. The highest peak, *La Puntita en Jayuya*, rises to a height of 4,398 feet, towering over the narrow, rich little valleys that interlace the mountains.

Encircling the island is an extensive coastal plain once used by early Spanish settlers as a grazing range for their cattle, but now largely given over to sugar cane plantations. The southern coastal plain must be irrigated, but

Some of the most beautiful and tranquil beaches in the world are to be found along Puerto Rico's shore line. This one, Point Caracoles, is located on the north coast.

Towering mountains are as much a part of island scenery as are palm-shaded beaches. Here, near Arecibo on the north coast, hulking mountains covered with greenery add majesty to the landscape.

elsewhere on the island the thousands of small streams that honeycomb the mountains provide a good water supply. The mountains themselves, once covered by tropical rain forests, are for the most part bare and rocky today, the result of centuries of erosion and extensive logging operations that, many years ago, produced cedar, ebony, magnolia, laurel, mahogany and West Indian sandalwood in great quantities. Today, however, the government is engaged in replanting forests on 100,000 acres of federally owned land.

Remains of the once lush rain forest can still be found at El Yunque National Forest, and in the valleys the vegetation is heavily verdant. Bamboo, tree ferns, orchids, palms and many flowering trees such as hibiscus and African tulip add vivid beauty to the island. Orange, mango, avocado, papaya and other fruit trees can be found growing wild. Bananas, pineapples, grapefruit, guavas and breadfruit are also grown in Puerto Rico. The valleys are planted with sugar cane and tobacco while the tillable slopes of the mountains are generally given over to coffee plantations. Along the coastal plains, white sand beaches graced by backdrops of tropical greenery curve in and out along the sea's edge. They provide some of the most beautiful facilities in the world for sun bathing and swimming.

The temperature is remarkably stable throughout the year, averaging about 75° in the winter and 80° in the summer. Although it is generally quite warm in the daytime, fresh breezes sweep down from the mountains to make the nights pleasantly cool.

Puerto Rico averages 65 inches of rain a year, more than falls in any part of the United States.

The rolling hills of Puerto Rico's interior sometimes reach heights of 3,000 feet above sea level. The lower slopes of these hills near Aibonito have been terraced and cultivated.

Summer and autumn are the rainy seasons, but most moisture comes in the form of light showers. It is a rare day when the sun does not shine at least part of the time. The island lies directly in the "hurricane belt" of the Caribbean, and hurricanes have more than once devastated the fields, ripped up the towns and sent tidal waves swirling over the beaches. Because of the advance warnings today available through meteorological equipment, precautions are now taken to keep damage at a minimum. Hurricanes are no longer the threat they once were.

The cities of Puerto Rico present a picturesque and unusual contrast between Old Spain and the modern world. Towering new buildings of steel and glass construction and the classical Spanish-Moorish architecture of Spain stand side by side. Wide traffic-controlled avenues intersect the many narrow, winding streets that meander through the older parts of Puerto Rico's cities.

San Juan, on the north coast, is the capital and largest city (population 500,000). Ponce (153,400) to the south and Mayagüez (94,000) to the west are the other principal cities. From these, the cities and towns range downwards in size to countless tiny villages tucked around the mountains of the interior. Many of these have less than 100 people.

Virtually every community on Puerto Rico can be reached either by car on the network of modern highways that spread across the island, or by the railway that circles it. Some 38 ship lines make Puerto Rico a regular port of call, and half a dozen airlines maintain regular schedules between the United States and the sprawling, modernistic airport outside of San Juan.

The road to the national rain forest, El Yunque, is lined with fantastic, varied tropical growth. Less than an hour's drive from the Isla Verde section of San Juan, El Yunque abounds with wild orchids, 30-foot tree ferns and many other beautiful rare trees. Both the Atlantic and the Caribbean can be seen from the highest point in the park.

(Above) More than 3,000 miles of modern roads wind through magnificent country in Puerto Rico's interior. Here travellers pause for a roadside picnic overlooking a valley farm. They are probably en route from San Juan to Ponce.

The sprawling, comfortable-looking hotel shown here is located on the slopes of the rugged hills that encircle a peaceful bay near Montemar.

22

From the walls of San Cristobal Castle, built by the Spanish on a high hill overlooking the present-day capital, this visitor has a perfect view of part of the city and coast of San Juan.

San Juan presents a constant contrast between the Old World and the New. Here a street of stairs runs beneath the balconies of Spanish-style houses. The street dates back to the 1500's, but the lights are electric.

(Above) Modern highways swirl into San Juan from all directions. Three bridges connect the little island of Old San Juan with Santurce, the city's business district. In the background is an arm of San Juan Bay.

(Below) Motorists travel quickly along the waterfront.

(Above) Over the centuries the crashing surf cut deep caves among these coastal rocks. In ancient times, the Indians of Puerto Rico lived in these caves, and traces of their civilization can still be found here.

(Right) This strange stone, not far from the Indian caves, seems to defy the law of gravity!

Members of the San Juan Ballet company make a dramatic tableau on the jagged rocks of the Indian caves near Arecibo.

3. THE PEOPLE

The Puerto Rican's racial make-up is diverse. Most Puerto Ricans are of Spanish descent, and though very few traces of Indian blood remain, intermarriage between whites and Negroes has been common since the first slaves arrived early in the 16th century. As the centuries went by, other races were added to the tiny island's heritage.

From Haiti and Santo Domingo (the Hispaniola of Columbus' time) came French families in 1801, fleeing the revolutionary and dictatorial government of Toussaint l'Ouverture, who had been named Haiti's president for life. From Louisiana in 1816 came 83 Americans who preferred a Roman Catholic Puerto Rico to a Protestant United States. From Venezuela came refugee Spanish royalists and from Philadelphia, strangely enough, came a large group of Irish Catholics. Puerto Ricans with red hair, fair skin and blue eyes are numerous around Castaner and Utuado in the island's interior.

Generally, the Puerto Rican tends to be slight of build and rather short, due in part to centuries of life in a land where malnutrition was common. Most Puerto Ricans are darker skinned than North Americans. The most startling difference between islanders and other American citizens, however, is their average age. Puerto Ricans are younger. Until recently, the lack of proper nutrition and adequate medical facilities kept the islander's life expectancy at a shockingly low figure.

As late as 1945, the census showed 76 per cent of the population was under 35 years of age. Even today, $1\frac{1}{2}$ million of a total population of 2.6 million are under 35. This aspect of island life is changing, however, thanks to the advent of modern medical science and to a tremendous improvement in living conditions. In 1940 the average Puerto Rican could expect to live only to the age of 46, but today he has a life expectancy of 70.

The gap between the wealthy aristocracy of Puerto Rico and the half-starving, bare-footed

On special occasions Puerto Rican girls dress in the costumes of their Spanish ancestors. With its bouffant net skirt and fitted lace bodice, the dress shown here would please any girl. But even more beautiful than the dress itself is the mantilla, *a headdress made of yards and yards of delicate lace.*

The captain of a Caribbean cargo schooner takes time out to relax on a San Juan pier.

jibaros, or peasants, who still make up the majority of the population, is gradually being bridged by a new industrial class. The industrial worker was virtually nonexistent twenty years ago, but with the introduction of modern manufacturing systems, the growing number of factories and the increased capital being poured into the island from businesses in the United States, the number of industrial and commercial workers has been expanding rapidly. It is in this hard-working, ambitious group that the Puerto Rican leaders have placed their hopes for future prosperity.

Generations are not required to raise the *jibaro's* economic and social status; he need only leave his *bohio* (palm-thatched hut) in the interior and get a job in a factory. Thousands are making the transition each year.

Eighty per cent of the Puerto Ricans are nominally Catholic, but, to quote the Bishop of San Juan, "only about 20 per cent of them are practising Catholics." Spiritualism holds a strong place in island beliefs and for the *jibaro,* the paganism of the ancestral Arawaks is still a powerful force, even though he probably has been formally baptized in the Catholic Church.

Protestantism, unknown on the island prior to its occupation by the North Americans, is fairly well represented, but on a strangely categorized basis. In order to prevent overlapping of effort, the first missionaries zoned the island by areas and today that zoning is still apparent. The Baptists occupy a broad diagonal strip that runs across the island from Ponce to San Juan. The Methodists are located in the north near Arecibo. The western end of the island is heavily Presbyterian, and the eastern end Congregationalist. The United Brethren are located on the south coast and the Episcopalians mainly in the large cities and suburbs.

The typical Puerto Rican is friendly but quite sensitive. He makes friends and offers his sympathy quickly. He is proud by nature, especially of his children. Family ties are strong in Puerto Rico, and the families are big. In fact, in many of the smaller villages, almost all the inhabitants are related. Children often rule their homes, for Puerto Rican parents willingly make sacrifices for them.

Although he uses his mother's name, the Puerto Rican is referred to by his father's. Thus Roberto Sanchez Vilella, the Governor, is called Sanchez. Vilella was his mother's maiden name.

EDUCATION

All Puerto Ricans speak Spanish and many of them also speak English. Spanish is the language of instruction in the schools, but English is taught and emphasized at all levels. This is a great improvement over the system which prevailed until 1948. At that time English was the official language of instruction, and was regarded as a symbol of colonialism. However, in 1948, the United States relinquished control of Puerto Rican education and permitted the governor to appoint a commissioner of education directly responsible to him and to the citizens of the island. From this point on, education has advanced rapidly.

School enrollment doubled between 1940 and 1957. Today 95 per cent of school-age children attend classes. The rate of literacy is 90 per cent, compared with 69 per cent in 1940. Perhaps the most dramatic indication of Puerto Rico's enthusiasm for education is the fact that

28

(Right) Tiny gemlike Santo Cristo Chapel in Old San Juan was built by order of the Spanish governor in 1752 to memorialize the miraculous escape from death of a young horseman who plunged over the wall of the city at this point. Located on one of the city's narrow old cobblestone streets, it has seats for only a dozen worshippers, although twice that number sometimes crowd inside.

(Below) The Union Church in San Juan is the epitome of modern architecture. It provides a striking contrast to the Spanish-Moorish buildings which are much more typical of the city.

29

The Plaza Principal *in San German is typical of those found in all the larger cities of Puerto Rico.*

in 1956 its government spent 29 per cent of its total budget on education—a proportion larger than that of any other country in the world except Israel.

Educational facilities also exist for adults who wish to learn English or who want to receive vocational training in fields ranging from mechanics to nursing. In both isolated and urban areas evening high schools, adult education projects and vocational training classes are available.

Puerto Rico is also proud of its three universities: Catholic University is located in Ponce. The University of Puerto Rico has most

31

This elaborate and intricately carved altar is so breathtaking that it dominates San José Church in Old San Juan.

Symbolic of the Spanish heritage of Puerto Rico is this serene plaza at Mayagüez, with Columbus' statue in the middle.

of its colleges at Río Piedras, the rest in Mayagüez. Founded in 1930, the university has grown to meet the needs of the island; there are 17 colleges, divisions and schools, providing instruction for more than 25,000 students. Many attend evening classes, because it is necessary for them to hold regular daytime jobs. Even in remote areas the university offers extension courses with special emphasis on teachers' training. The Inter-American University with an enrollment of 5,500 is located at San German.

(Right) The Cathedral of Our Lady of Guadalupe represents the Old World style. It dominates the main plaza of Ponce, Puerto Rico's second largest city.

33

(*Above*) *Puerto Rico is trying to make the decade of the 1960's a time for "a great enterprise" in education, in and out of the school. By far the largest item in the Commonwealth's budget is education, with between 30 and 35 cents of each dollar being spent toward that end. Schools such as this, the new De Hostos High School in Mayagüez, are now being constructed throughout the island. Puerto Rico's literacy rate is 90 per cent and still rising.*

(*Left*) *Former Governor Luís Muñoz Marín dedicating WIPR-TV, an educational station operated by the Department of Education of the Commonwealth.*

(Right) It's an old Spanish custom to trim trees in public squares with horticultural haircuts. These trees in the plaza at Caguas, near San Juan, grow so thick that the sun cannot filter through their leaves. The result is a mushroom-shaped umbrella that provides perfect shade.

(Below) On special occasions, the young women of San Juan don the costumes and mantillas of Old Spain to recreate the atmosphere of an earlier era in Puerto Rico's history.

Secluded, graceful and cool balconies, such as this, are easy to find in the middle of Old San Juan. This is a beautifully restored hotel called El Convento (because it was formerly a convent) which illustrates the delicacy of Spanish design.

Festivals often liven up the streets of San Juan. Perhaps the most elaborate is the San Juan Bautista Carnival, held in June to extol the capital's patron saint. During the Carnival it is not unusual to see a dragon caught in a traffic jam!

RECREATION

Puerto Ricans love sports, particularly horse racing, basketball, cockfighting and baseball.

Gambling is popular, too; the national lottery is a considerable source of income for the island. Anywhere, any time, a cockfight is bound to draw an excited crowd, and good fighting birds are only a little bit less well known than outstanding baseball players.

The young people have a special form of relaxation. During pleasantly cool evenings, they dress in their finest, most colorful clothes and promenade through the streets of their towns. Sometimes they end up at a theatre; in Puerto Rico Mexican and Argentine pictures rival American films in popularity.

Making handicrafts is another popular pastime. Most Puerto Ricans are deft at using their hands, and it is amazing what useful objects they can make from whatever is available—native woods, seeds, clays and fibres. No matter how simple or poor, a Puerto Rican home is decorated with handmade pottery, straw rugs, baskets and table mats. Practically all the women are expert at needlework, for they are taught this art from the time they are

(Right) Taking part in the Children's Parade at the Carnival of San Juan Bautista is this bullfighter, marching proudly down the street with his lady.

Masquerade parties and street dancing are part of the Carnival celebration, but the highlight is the Children's Parade.

children. Her fine embroidery is a special source of pride to every Puerto Rican woman. Their skill at hand work has made Puerto Ricans valuable workers at today's machine-worked embroidery.

THE CULTURE

Not only does the heritage of Old Spain make itself felt in the language and architecture of Puerto Rico, it is also the dominant factor in the island's culture. The Spanish influence is everywhere—in the music, the art, the drama and the literature of the island. And from the Spanish, too, come the many fiestas that are such an integral and joyful part of Puerto Rican life. The feast days of the Catholic Church are widely observed and more often than not are the occasion for city- or village-wide celebrations, pageants and parades.

The Fiesta of St. John the Baptist, for whom the island was originally named by Columbus, is one of the most enthusiastically celebrated festivals of the year. For several days before and after the actual date, June 24, there are parties, carnivals, dances and music in the gaily decorated plazas. On the night of the 23rd, thousands of families keep all-night vigils before open bonfires on the beaches. At dawn, they wade into the water in a symbolical re-enactment of the baptism of Christ. This act of piety, according to Puerto Rican tradition, assures the islanders of good health for the coming year.

Each town has its own patron saint and each saint's day is another occasion for a long, loud and happy festival. There are always special masses in the churches on a saint's day, and often a procession of worshippers will wind through the streets carrying candles, holy relics and statues.

At Christmas, the Puerto Ricans manage to combine Spanish and American customs with some that are native to the island. As a result, the Christmas season lasts all the way from early December through January 8. Children receive gifts on both *Nochebuena* (Christmas Eve) and on Three Kings' Day (Epiphany), January 6. Santa Claus takes care of the gift-giving on *Nochebuena*. On Three Kings' Day excited children put boxes of fresh grass under their beds for the camels of the Magi. Next morning the delighted youngsters discover that the grass has been eaten and toys and confectionery left in its place.

Throughout the Christmas season, groups of singers and musicians wander from house

(Above) A Teatro Rodante, *"theatre on wheels," brings plays and musicals to Puerto Rico's rural towns and villages. This travelling theatre is sponsored by the University of Puerto Rico. Under faculty direction, university students design and build sets, handle the staging and perform in the theatre's productions. Shown here is a scene from "The Puppets of Cachiporra," by Garcia Lorca, the world-renowned Spanish poet.*

(Right) In any Puerto Rican village a visit from the Theatre on Wheels is an exciting event. These young-sters are taking no chance of not getting front-row seats.

One of the island's most beloved figures is Pablo Casals, famous Spanish cellist and the founder of the Commonwealth's Symphony Orchestra, who now makes his home in San Juan.

to house singing *villancicos*, or Christmas carols. Traditional Christmas dishes include *arroz con dulce* (a sweet rice pudding), different kinds of sausages, *pasteles* (a banana paste mixed with chopped meat and wrapped in plantain leaves), and most delicious of all, *lechón asado* (lean pig roasted whole over a bed of glowing charcoal).·

Music is the art which flourishes best in Puerto Rico. Musical expression ranges in sophistication from the simple songs of the roaming street singers, who come out in large numbers during Christmas and other holiday seasons, to the symphonic works performed during the renowned Casals Festival. The great cellist Pablo Casals, a Spaniard, came in 1956 to make his home in Puerto Rico, the island of his mother's birth. It was Casals, at 84, who established the Puerto Rico Symphony Orchestra and the Commonwealth Conservatory for Puerto Ricans who wish to study music. The Casals Festival, held each spring, is one of the best known musical events in the world. It has brought to the island such musicians as Isaac Stern, Jan Peerce, Alexander Schneider and Eugene Aistomin.

The Puerto Rican government, which has been working so hard to improve the economic and political status of the island, has also taken organized steps to raise the cultural standards of its citizens. Under a project called *Operación Serenidad* (Operation Serenity), a travelling library goes from town to town, a mobile museum makes the rounds of the island and a theatre on wheels brings drama to the *jíbaro's* out-of-the-way village.

(Below) Puerto Rico's new Symphony Orchestra, organized by Pablo Casals, drew a crowd of almost 4,000 when it gave its first outdoor concert in the north coast city of Arecibo. The 42 members of the orchestra performed works by Mozart, Mendelssohn, Johann Strauss and a Puerto Rican composer, Hector Campos Parsi. Alexander Schneider was the guest conductor, and Maria Esther Robles the soprano soloist.

41

This 19th-century Spanish-style building in Old San Juan is the headquarters of Puerto Rico's Institute of Culture. Among other things, the Institute supervises the restoration of all historic monuments. Staff members search for and discover ancient Indian relics. Their activities include sponsoring art, metal work and graphic art displays as well as cultural expositions from other lands.

One of the most effective agencies of *Operación Serenidad* is the Institute of Puerto Rican Culture. It was established in 1955 to study, promote and preserve the island's traditional culture, and it has founded offices throughout the island for these purposes. The Institute sponsors concerts, lectures, ballets, art exhibits, plays and films. The *Casa del Libro*, literally "House of the Book," in Old San Juan contains nearly 200 books printed before 1501.

As in Spain, the most popular form of literary expression in Puerto Rico is poetry. Today the island has many poets, several of whom are famous in the Spanish-speaking world. The best-known are probably Luís Lloréns Torres and Luís Palés Matos.

Puerto Rico has also produced fine actors (for example, José Ferrer and Juano Hernandez), as well as opera stars of the stature of Graciela Rivera and Justino Diaz.

HOUSING

In any small country in which overpopulation and mass poverty go hand in hand, housing is a serious problem, and so it is in Puerto Rico. Today, however, *bohíos*—the palm-thatched cabins built on stilts—and the zinc and wood shacks of the urban poor are rapidly disappearing. The problem is being solved in a unique manner. The government supplies materials and technical aid to families grouped into home-building cooperatives. The cooperative members then do the actual construction themselves. Of the 60,000 houses built between 1950 and 1960, 10,000 were put up in this manner.

The self-help house is made of reinforced concrete or concrete blocks and consists of a living room, two bedrooms and a kitchen. The cost is only $350 (£125) and is paid in small monthly installments over periods up to ten years. In another plan to clear the island's slums, the government is building massive low-rent apartment blocks, with rents assigned in accordance with the ability of the head of the house to pay. An apartment for a family with seven children is as little as $6.50 (£2-6s) a month. Puerto Rican housing planners are confident that by 1970 most of the slum areas will have been replaced by attractive, low-cost housing.

THE MIGRANTS

In spite of Puerto Rico's rapid economic progress, there are still too few jobs for an increasing population. This situation, combined with the fact that wages are higher on the mainland, has drawn many Puerto Ricans to the United States. There are an estimated 900,000 Puerto Ricans in the United States now, all but about 200,000 of them in New York City. Because of improved conditions on the island, numerous Puerto Ricans are returning—in fact, more returned in 1964 than migrated to the U.S.

Many new apartments and houses are being built under public housing, one of the government's most successful plans.

Three housing developments are included in this shot taken from the air just outside the San Juan metropolitan area. Housing is a major problem in Puerto Rico, but with the growth of such projects as these, it is gradually being solved.

Another group, estimated at some 200,000 a year, goes to the United States yearly to work on farms in the East and Midwest during the harvest season. Then they return to the island to help handle the Puerto Rican sugar harvest.

The island government neither encourages nor discourages its citizens from going to the "States," but once they have migrated, they find that the Commonwealth has established agencies in New York and eleven other cities to help them get settled as quickly as possible.

Most Puerto Rican women employed in New York City work in the needle trades. Skill at hand-needlework makes them especially gifted at machine operation. Probably the major source of employment for the men are the hotel

and restaurant industries, but large numbers also work for various manufacturing companies and in hospitals.

Puerto Ricans who move to the United States have to face the same social barriers which confronted newcomers from other countries in the past. Cultural differences and language problems present serious difficulties, and Puerto Ricans who are also Negroes have to surmount the additional obstacle of color discrimination. Prejudice based on skin color is a new situation for the Puerto Rican; on the island whites and Negroes have lived peacefully together for four centuries. As a result, only 8 per cent of Puerto Rican migrants are Negro even though 20 per cent of the island's total population is Negro. The difficulties resulting from color discrimination are multiplied by the fact that Puerto Rican Negroes in the United States sometimes deliberately speak Spanish in order to keep from being identified with American Negroes, hoping to avoid the barriers set up in many cities.

Despite their difficulties as newcomers, Puerto Ricans are contributing a great deal besides a work-force to the United States. Their attitude of racial tolerance is far in advance of mainland practice. The stability of their family group deserves admiration. Puerto Ricans are typically non-materialistic and fun-loving. Perhaps most important, they tend to form their opinions of others according to what a person is, not by what he possesses.

A recent addition to the island's largest industrial sector, this tricot mill in Arecibo manufactures nylon and acetates. Puerto Rico's apparel and textile industry comprises over 400 plants, and shipments to the U.S. of apparel products have more than doubled in the last nine years to more than $190 (£68) million.

La Fortalez, Puerto Rico's executive mansion, has been the home of its governors for over 400 years. When it was built in 1533, it was intended as a fortress to guard the Bay of San Juan. Later it was found that the site was completely inadequate for defence and the building was turned into a residence for the island's governors.

4. THE GOVERNMENT

The Commonwealth of Puerto Rico has a modern, efficient representative government regulated by the traditional checks and balances characteristic of the United States, but flexible enough to provide for changes required to meet future conditions, whether they be economic, political or social.

This governmental set-up was not arrived at easily. When the Americans took over in 1898, they moved in with a high-handed autocratic form of colonial government that may well have been more restrictive than that which Puerto Ricans would have had under the constitution wrested from Spain only a year previously. In 1900, the U.S. Congress passed the Foraker Act, guaranteeing military protection for the island and setting up a House of Representatives, the delegates of which were to be elected by the Puerto Ricans themselves.

Through a remarkable bit of political ambiguity, however, the same act virtually eliminated any possibility of home rule. The governor, the heads of the six top administrative departments and the members of the upper house of the Puerto Rican Legislature—the Executive Council—were all appointed by the

46

The crystal chandelier over the governor's desk in La Fortalez is one of the smallest wild-life refuges in the world. The small tangle of twigs and weeds near the top of the chandelier is a bird's nest. Governor Muñoz put out an official decree protecting the bird after its invasion was discovered.

President of the United States. Puerto Ricans were not required to pay federal income taxes, as they are today, but their delegate to the U.S. House of Representatives was given no vote. For all practical purposes, Puerto Rico was treated as a "poor-cousin" possession.

Reform was slow in coming but, in 1917, pressed by a rising desire for independence on the island, Congress passed the Jones Act, which granted U.S. citizenship to all Puerto Ricans and set up a bicameral legislature to be elected by the islanders. The governor, key members of the cabinet and Supreme Court justices were still appointed by the President, however.

For Puerto Rico, the Jones Act did not establish a fully benevolent political structure. The United States had poured money into

Luis Muñoz Marín was the first governor freely chosen by Puerto Ricans, and served continuously, 1948-64. It was his conception of economic and social reform, "Operation Bootstrap," that was basically responsible for the tremendous strides Puerto Rico has made to eliminate poverty and raise its standard of living.

developing the sugar industry and had raised the island's standard of living a bit. It had done little else, however, and by the mid-1930's even that advancement began to backfire. Despite a Foraker Act provision restricting corporations from holding more than 500 acres of land each, four corporations controlled more than 176,000 acres. Land reform was to become a major issue, and from this issue came Puerto Rico's present form of government.

What the Puerto Ricans needed was a dynamic, dedicated leader. They found him in Luís Muñoz Marín, whose father had led the island towards political freedom late in the 19th century. Muñoz, who spent many years in the United States formulating his political philosophy, first came to prominence in 1932 when he was elected Senator-at-Large to the Puerto Rican Legislature. In 1938, he organized the

Popular Democratic Party (*Populares*) with a platform emphasizing economic reconstruction and agrarian reform. Running on a promise to better the living conditions of the poverty-stricken *jíbaros*, or peasants, the *Populares* swept the island election in 1940.

Then the *Populares*, working closely with Governor Rexford Guy Tugwell, formerly Assistant Secretary of Agriculture in President Franklin D. Roosevelt's cabinet, set out to do what they had promised. They set up an industrial planning board, a transportation authority and a housing authority. Civil service was strengthened and the water resources authority reorganized. For the first time, the United States enforced that section of the Foraker Act limiting corporations and partnerships to 500 acres of Puerto Rican land. Gradually, under this project of "Operation

Bootstrap," as the *Populares* dubbed their economic reorganization plan, the island began to struggle out from under the oppressive weight of poverty. And, as the Puerto Ricans themselves began to better their own economic situation, their political situation improved. On August 5, 1947, President Harry S. Truman signed a bill creating the Commonwealth of Puerto Rico. Although the last stages of the plan to establish the Commonwealth did not become final until July 25, 1952, when it was ratified by the islanders themselves, Truman's action gave Puerto Rico true independence for the first time. Muñoz was elected Governor in 1948 and then re-elected in 1952, 1956 and 1960.

Today the Legislative Assembly consists of a Senate and House of Representatives, whose members are elected by direct vote every four years. Eight senatorial districts elect two Senators each and 40 representative districts one Representative each. Eleven Senators and eleven Representatives are elected on an at-large basis. Puerto Rico has a resident commissioner in the U.S. Congress who is allowed to give advice and recommendations but cannot vote. The islanders hold American citizenship but cannot vote in national elections unless they move to the United States, where they then come under local laws.

Executive power is vested in a governor elected by direct vote. There are eight executive departments, each headed by a secretary appointed by the governor. The Secretaries of

This is the interior of the Puerto Rican House of Representatives. There are three major political parties, the Popular Democratic Party, which is currently in power and is a strong champion of the Commonwealth set-up; the Statehood Party, which seeks statehood; and the Independent Party, which wants complete independence from the United States.

49

(*Left*) *Several women occupy important governmental posts in Puerto Rico. Shown on the left is Mrs. Petroamerica Pagan de Colón, Director of the Bureau of Employment Security of the Department of Labor.*

State, Justice, Education, Health, Treasury, Labor, Agriculture and Commerce and Public Works make up the Governor's cabinet. The judiciary system is similar to that of the United States. It consists of a Supreme Court and a complex network of lower courts.

(*Below*) *Doña Felisa Rincon de Gautier, Mayoress of San Juan, is presented with a bouquet of roses by the Boy Scouts. In 1954 she was named "Woman of the Americas."*

(*Above*) *In the city of Ponce, the vivid* Parque de Bombas (*firehouse*) *painted in bold red and black stripes and ornamented with bright green and yellow designs, is one of Puerto Rico's most photographed buildings.*

(*Right*) *The graceful modernism of the Supreme Court Building in San Juan offers a striking contrast to the Old Spanish style of La Fortaleza and the granite massiveness of El Morro.*

The busy San Juan sea front includes a drydock and a marine terminal. Shown here is the largest commercial drydock in the Caribbean.

5. THE ECONOMY

Twenty years ago, Puerto Rico was known as "the pesthole of the Caribbean." There was virtually no money for investment and development on the island, there was a serious lack of natural resources for manufacturing, disease was widespread and 31 per cent of the population was illiterate.

Today there is still poverty in Puerto Rico, but it is rapidly decreasing; by 1975 it is expected to be almost completely wiped out. Though in 1940, Puerto Rico could list bank assets amounting to only 93 million dollars, by 1964 that figure had grown to $1.4 billion. There are over 2,000 factories in operation now as compared to a few hundred in 1940. Of the two most ravaging diseases, malaria is today almost nonexistent and the incidence of tuberculosis has been drastically reduced.

These advances are the direct results of a meticulously planned, daringly conceived project: Operation Bootstrap.

Operation Bootstrap is the outgrowth of Governor Muñoz' scheme of economic and social reconstruction. It was designed by Puerto Ricans for Puerto Rico. Muñoz realized that if the island, a much neglected United States possession in 1940, was going to advance economically, the islanders themselves would have to do it. Thus was Operation Bootstrap conceived—and it has been amazingly successful.

The first step was the creation of a Planning Board in 1942 to serve as a clearing house and an organizing agency for the entire self-help project. It is the Planning Board that decides on priorities, sets up specific goals and generally administers one of the most startling economic upsurges in history. The actual details of the scheme are handled by three subsidiary boards,

the Water Resources Authority, the Government Development Bank and the Economic Development Administration.

The Water Resources Authority has provided the physical basis for economic development, that is, the construction and development of a power system, without which the industrialization of the island would be impossible. In 1964, more than 3 billion kilowatt hours of electrical energy were produced, and this figure is expected to double about every four years until 1975. In 1940, electrical output was only 130 million kilowatt hours.

The Government Development Bank is primarily concerned with the government's fiscal arrangements. It supervises loans by the government to private industry, acting as a negotiation agent for private investors. It has been particularly effective in spurring private builders to produce large-scale housing projects for low- and middle-income families.

Perhaps the most important agency, however, is the Economic Development Administration, known to Puerto Ricans as *Fomento* (meaning promotion, encouragement or aid). *Fomento* is the promotional arm of the government and the one which, sometimes by unusual means, is responsible for the great flow of private capital into the island.

Fomento began by building and operating factories until they were well established, then selling them to private investors. It obtained sweeping tax exemptions for industry, and then concentrated on promoting the island as a good site for factories to outside manufacturers. In order to bring in the industry it wanted, *Fomento* has been willing to make economic studies, locate plant sites, arrange for the construction of buildings, provide engineering and marketing

advice and, in some cases, even train the personnel.

Fomento's success has been remarkable. Today in Puerto Rico, branches of American corporations are manufacturing containers, textiles, fasteners, men's wear, abrasives, cigars, wiring devices, paper, infants' wear, shoes, lingerie, flour, pharmaceuticals, copper wire, television sets, hosiery, glycols, optical lenses, gloves, light metres, insecticides, precision bearings, transistors and cameras.

By 1975, *Fomento* hopes to have established 2,500 factories, employing 255,000 people, in Puerto Rico. Large shopping areas are being built everywhere on the island, and supermarkets, dress shops, drug stores and branches of various American chain stores are becoming commonplace. Oil companies are drilling and refineries are in operation. High quality marble, limestone, gypsum and industrially valuable sands and clays have also been discovered. Puerto Rico's present economic activity is a

One of the most charming beaches is mile-long Luquillo Beach at the eastern end of the island. Only an hour's drive from San Juan, it is a popular site for week-end swimming and picnics and includes an excellent anchorage for visiting boatmen.

striking contrast to its former purely agricultural economy.

Of major importance to Puerto Rico is its booming tourist trade. The year-round sunshine, great white sand beaches and the tropical loveliness of most of the island attracts more than 600,000 visitors a year and brings in more than $110 million annually. This industry, one of the prime concerns of *Fomento*, is expected to reach $150 million in the next five years and $200 million in the next ten.

The Caribe Hilton, one of the most lavishly appointed hotels in the Western Hemisphere, was built by the government at a cost of over

$7 million and then leased to the Hilton International Corporation to manage. Opened in 1949, it paid back the government's entire investment by 1957. Today, hotels and resort facilities abound along the beaches and in the mountains. The range as to price and type of accommodation available is wide. Most resorts offer reduced rates in the summer and early autumn.

The rapid growth of manufacturing and tourism in Puerto Rico has turned the continental United States and its island affiliate into mutually good customers. Puerto Ricans buy more, on a per capita basis, from the United States than do Canadians, and the island's purchases from America surpass those of such a booming country as Brazil: more than $1.1 billion a year.

Puerto Rico benefits too, for the United States is, in turn, the island's best customer, spending more than $850 million annually for Puerto Rican produce and goods. This is a rise of almost 200 per cent since 1953. Puerto Rico is also a good customer for Britain. Exports to Britain in 1963 amounted to £704,485 and imports £2,653,702.

Inspired by Governor Muñoz Marín's concept of Operation Bootstrap, now administered by Governor Sanchez, Puerto Ricans are making their island one of the busiest, most productive and most attractive in the world.

San Juan's "Gold Coast" (the Condado Beach section) has some of the most luxurious and newest hotels in the Caribbean. From left to right in "hotel row" are the La Concha, Condado Beach Hotel, San Jerónimo Hilton and Caribe Hilton.

(Above) The design of this strangely shaped hotel in San Juan, the Normandie, is patterned after that of the famous French luxury liner.

(Left) These odd little boats may look like sea-going golf carts, but they provide quick transportation for guests of the Escambron Beach Hotel.

(Right) The tobacco-growing region is in the eastern part of the island. Farmers have to work on slopes so steep that they sometimes rope themselves together like mountain climbers. Puerto Rico's tobacco is used as the filler in cigars.

(Below) The backbone of the Puerto Rican economy is sugar cane, from which sugar and rum are made. This is a typical scene showing cane-cutters trimming the stalks with machetes.

(Above) A sugar refinery, Central Machete, near Guayama, is surrounded by fields of cane.

(Left) A scheme of hydroponics has been launched successfully by Puerto Rico's Land Authority. Here is a view of a farm where tomato plants are cultivated in gravel beds, nourished primarily by chemically treated water.

(Above) The drive to modernize Puerto Rico's farming industry has resulted in agricultural fairs such as this one at Bayamon, where visitors can see the latest farm machinery.

(Below) The pineapple harvest is a slow, laborious operation. Each piece of fruit must be cut from the plant by hand. Workers take the fruit from the fields in baskets carried on their heads.

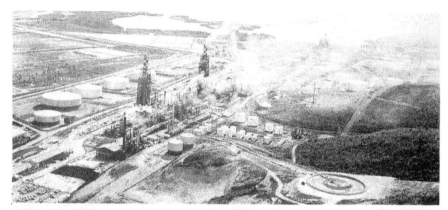

Having almost no natural resources, Puerto Rico has had to buy them from other countries. Crude oil is imported and refined by the Commonwealth Refinery, shown here, and is then used as fuel for electric power plants.

Every phase of the sugar industry except harvesting is mechanized. Here sugar is being loaded into rail cars at dockside.

This glittering structure is not part of an amusement park, as it might seem at first glance, but the Puerto Nuevo steam power plant located at San Juan.

(Left) The Puerto Rican Water Resources Authority uses helicopters to erect transmission poles. In 15 days, 119 poles were put up by this method, a job that would have taken ground crews 5 months to complete.

(Below) At the Carborundum Company of Puerto Rico, located in Mayagüez, a worker examines an enormous kiln in which grinding stones are processed. This factory produces seals for electronic parts, capacitors and printed circuits.

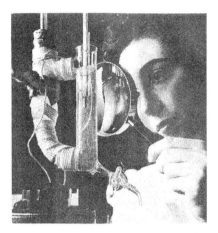

(Above) This girl is a worker in a plant which produces transistors.

(Above) This woman works in the rapidly expanding steroids manufacturing industry.

The two masked workers behind the glass are not spacemen, but actually supervising the manufacture of special drug products in the isolation room of a Puerto Rico factory where more than 300 people are employed.

63

(Above) These apartment houses in San Juan's Condado Beach section are operated on a co-operative basis. Since tenants own their own apartments, they can sell them any time.

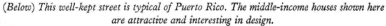

(Below) This well-kept street is typical of Puerto Rico. The middle-income houses shown here are attractive and interesting in design.

puertoricoinpict00ster

puertoricoinpict00ster

puertoricoinpict00ster

CPSIA information can be obtained
at www.ICGtesting.com
Printed in the USA
BVHW041250020322
630458BV00002BA/8

9 781013 430718